STAYING

~ IN THE ~

LIGHT

A 7-WEEK DEVOTIONAL STUDY GUIDE

STAYING IN THE LIGHT

Copyright © by **MARIAN OWONIYI 2023**

marian.owbooks@gmail.com

ISBN:

Edited by Ruthless Editing
+44 782 871 3245

Cover Design & Layout: Chaptr10
chaptr10publish@gmail.com
+234 812 493 5612

CHAPTR 10

STAYING
~ IN THE ~
LIGHT

A 7-WEEK DEVOTIONAL STUDY GUIDE

MARIAN OWONIYI

"Though I am the least deserving of all God's people, he graciously gave me the privilege of telling the gentiles about the endless treasures available to them in Christ"

(Ephesians 3:8, NLT).

Contents

Fulfilling Purpose: **Birthing This Guide**

WHAT IS PURPOSE?

Purpose is how you fit into the grand scheme of God's plan. The reason you were made. The motive behind and essence of your creation. Therefore, we know purpose cannot be what you have manoeuvred yourself into, whether by way of occupation or other means. With purpose, it is never too early to begin fulfilling it, rather it gets *'later'* for every moment spent not living it.

Imagine knitting a jumper but not putting it to use in a constantly cold geographical location or trying to use it as a pair of trousers. It will be extremely ill-fitting.

You might convince yourself that it is keeping part of your legs warm; however, it is not being used appropriately and, therefore, not making the difference it was made for, which is to be worn to cover your upper body and retain heat to keep most parts of your body warm.

Purpose can come with sacrifice, but it ultimately creates a lasting impact not just on yourself but on all who come in contact with you directly or indirectly.

For a long time, I wondered about my purpose. What was I made for? What impact have I been created to make on this earth? I tried searching with human wisdom and realised that gave no direction, so I began to seek God for the answer to my wonderment.

The urge grew and I became desperate to know and fulfil my purpose. My satisfaction was no longer in the things I was chasing. I was no longer fulfilled with manoeuvring my life in the way I saw fit or in a way I thought would bring fulfilment. I needed God to help me. I needed to 'enter in', to enter into purpose.

Time was going; the little babe of yesterday was now a grown woman and there was no longer time for excuses. I had squandered enough time, but I still have some strong years ahead to give to the Lord.

I did not want to discover purpose on my dying bed or when my bones were tired. I wanted to live for Elohim.

Not as a Sunday Christian, a church worker, or even as one seen as being on fire for Him. Now, all these are good but for me, were not enough if I was not used for the purpose I was made. I needed to live in line with my *'instruction manual'*. I was gaining spiritual hypersensitivity to the number of my days and needed a divinely wise heart to make my existence what it ought to be.

For a long time, I had the revelation that I was made to worship Him. I carried this in my heart and sometimes wondered, Aren't we all made to worship Him? My heart was not quite *'opened'* to understand that we were each made to worship Him in our own specific way because we are all unique in how we've been 'wonderfully and fearfully' made. Like the body of Christ has many members with different functions but remains one body, we are also made with giftings peculiar to each of us but ultimately meant to glorify God in our worship of Him.

There was a burning desire within me to share Jesus with the world. I wanted to share the realness of our God with a world to which he seemed abstract. I wanted everyone to know Him, to get a chance to encounter the Almighty God.

I wanted the world to desire a relationship with Him, for each person to know Jesus for themself. My heart yearned for this and my Spirit wanted to shout, 'Can you not see that He is real? He is alive and desires a relationship with you; to know you and reveal Himself to you; to heal you and make your life new again'. My Spirit had so much desire, but my flesh hardly showed evidence of this.

My body kept busy, going through the routine of life with increasing dissatisfaction. I began to have some clarity that telling others about Jesus was my unique way of worship.

This was not my only way to worship but the way I was called to worship Elohim. This was a snippet of revelation, and I needed more. I wanted the whole picture but deep within me, I knew I needed to take a step of faith. I needed clarity on which direction to go with this first step. I did not have a natural desire to stand on a stage, holding a microphone to preach.

I made excuses for every avenue that seemed like a public commitment, until I began to write down the words dropped into my heart. I needed people to know about Jesus, even if it was through reading about Him. I wrote but delayed getting it to a platform that would allow the world to read and learn more about Him.

The burden to share the gospel of Jesus Christ grew bigger, and I knew I was letting down those waiting to hear or read what I had written. I felt the Lord had taken me thus far, but I was distracted by other opportunities whilst trying to convince myself they were avenues by which God could use me to fulfil purpose. It soon became clear that I had detoured from the heavenly satnav's direction and needed the Holy Spirit to reroute my directions.

I felt lost, frustrated, tired, and desperate for precise instructions. I was ready to give up my own way for His way but was not investing time into seeking His will for direction. Life's routine kept me occupied and even when mercy allowed for time, I kept myself busy with nothing.

I couldn't proceed forward, neither could I go back. I dared not take any sideway detour without clear instructions, yet no new revelations seemed to be coming through. I was tired and felt weak in my spirit.

I was desperate not to continue life outside the will of God. I wanted the words I had been inspired to write to be in people's hands and be read—for them to discover Christ for themselves—but felt helpless. I kept trying to come up with ideas, knowing that was not the way. I seemed to have forgotten how to let go and let God have His way in my life. My lips spoke the words 'I surrender'.

My spirit was desperate for God to take control but there was a battle of wills going on in my soul. I needed divine intervention. I prayed to God to give me clarity of purpose and help me fulfil my purpose.

I knew that quality time in His presence was required. I needed to slow down and spend time with my maker, the one with my instruction manual. I cried out for Jesus to intercede for me. I was fast losing motivation on things outside of Him, yet I had no idea which way to turn. I wanted people to know of Him, but where do I begin? I wanted to be away by myself in a place where all I did was listen to words from the Holy Scriptures, the Bible.

I wanted time to focus on Him and hear from Him, but life's practicalities stood in the way. Every second out of purpose ticked louder as I desperately waited for help to appear. I wanted to preach now; I was happy to speak but asked myself 'Where is the crowd? Who is listening? Where is the avenue?' I didn't want to copy others. The fear of doing it my own way set in and I began to second-guess every idea.

'Start from where you are'. The words were so silent I could have almost missed it. In fact, I partially dismissed it. This was the intermittent whisper coming through as I typed words on my laptop. *'Start from where you are'*. 'But Lord, where am I? I feel so lost, so out of line from your will that I do not even know where to begin. Is that even you? I'm sorry for doubting as I know it is you, but fear was rearing its ugly head.' I was puzzled and whispered to the Lord to remove all spirits of confusion from me.

The question of 'where I was' remained. I do, however, know that I was at the point of no longer wanting to chase shadows. I was no longer interested in what the world had to offer but what God desired of me.

Therefore, whether through a Christian podcast, Holy-Spirit-inspired writings, a church platform or whatever means was presented, I was ready to start from where I was. I gained an understanding that 'where I was' was related to the book I had written but never published—the writings the world was waiting to read but which I had withheld for two years.

I now understood that the Lord had been leading me until I decided to take a detour. And now, He awaits at the point of His last directions. His direction was to write the vision down and, moving forward, to send the word out into the world. Romans chapter 10 from verse 14 of the New King James Bible says, *'How then shall they call on Him in whom they have not believed? And how shall they believe in Him of whom they have not heard? And how shall they hear without a preacher?'*

I am by no means the worthiest, but the mercy and grace of God prevailed with reassuring words that say, 'Though I am the least deserving of all God's people, he graciously gave me the privilege of telling the gentiles about the endless treasures available to them in Christ' *(Ephesians 3:8, NLT)*. I pray you encounter Jesus Christ in a new dimension as you read this book.

How to Use This Devotional

This devotional study guide uses seven topics to help you gain an in-depth knowledge of God and His desires for you so you can live in the centre of His will. Study and meditate on one topic each week over seven weeks. This will allow you time to study and meditate deeply on each topic, ultimately equipping you to pray scripture-based prayers while understanding God better and experiencing His diverse manifestations.

At the end of every week, reflect on how studying the week's topic has made a difference. Record your reflections or testimonies in the space provided at the end of this book or in a journal. In the future, these will serve as a reminder of how far God has brought you.

The topics covered are not exhaustive but highlight typical circumstances that challenge mankind's ability to come into or remain in the light of God.

They will enlighten you on the reality of battles faced in such situations, prayerfully opening your eyes to the importance of our utmost dependence on Jehovah Elohim.

'This is the message we heard from Jesus and now declare to you: God is light, and there is no darkness in him at all. So we are lying if we say we have fellowship with God but go on living in spiritual darkness; we are not practicing the truth. But if we are living in the light, as God is in the light, then we have fellowship with each other, and the blood of Jesus, his Son, cleanses us from all sin.' (**1 John 1: 5-7, NLT**)

✚

Week

1

Stay in the Light

When you're in darkness, you may feel you are alone. You cannot see anything around you, but your life might appear to be going in the right direction—whether wrong or not. You adjust to the darkness and may even try to feel your way around. You start to feel comfortable in the darkness, not seeing anything wrong with you.

However, the moment that light comes, it's dazzling, even overwhelming at first. You feel exposed. Your eyes accustom, and you begin to see yourself, truly see yourself for who you are. You become aware of your surroundings. You start to realise that you are not alone. In fact, you are in the midst of a battle—a battle to keep people in the dark. A battle where those in the light seem under attack.

When you stop looking around and look back to the source of the light, the battlefield seems to fade away. Your fears and shame are gone. You do not feel alone any longer.

You realise the battle is actually not yours and hand it over to the one who has shone His light upon you. He fills you up and helps you realise you are greater than any attacker. You know you are strengthened and can do all things through the Almighty.

As children of the Most High God, we sometimes feel that our *'battles'* began when we gave our lives to Jesus Christ. We think we were doing OK, coasting through life before Jesus saved us, when really, we had no direction. We were wandering in the dark and oppressed by the heaviness in it.

For some, it's tempting to run back to the darkness to avoid the attacks—an expected reaction to a perceived inability to handle what seems a challenge greater than one can bear.

Remember the children of Israel in **Exodus 14:10-12**; they came out of the oppression in Egypt, looked back when they reached the Red Sea and saw a *'revelation'* of their enemy which drove terror into them. With this came unbelief, because fear and faith cannot occupy the same space.

The children of Israel would have rather stayed under Egyptian oppression than face their enemy when they felt exposed in the desert, even though God was guiding them through his prophet.

I have gone through times where I have felt the Lord asking me to leave a present situation and venture into something different. Sometimes, fear held me back and deprived me of the successes that awaited.

I gradually began to learn from some biblical characters, such as Abram, who in **Genesis chapter 12** was called out of what he had always known into the unknown. His obedience brought about a name change (to Abraham), many blessings from which we still benefit today, and much more.

I slowly but surely began to learn to take that step of faith and trusted God's guidance even when my daily reality made such steps of faith seem impossible.

Every time I have trusted the Lord and followed His leading, I have had more peace and progress, as I see all things working together for the good of my family and me.

Running back into darkness is running back into chains that bind, into a great blindfold, and into eternal damnation if mercy does not prevail.

We are not to fight our battles. **Psalm 44:6-7:** we are not to trust in our bow and sword but to rely on God. Do not fall for the enemy's game of peek-a-boo; it is a tactical game of instilling sudden fear. In this game, the enemy's true face is hidden, and he makes a sudden loud noise to pull down your guard.

The enemy specialises in counterfeiting; he is aware of what happened in **Jericho in Joshua chapter 6, verse 20.** He will make noises to strip down your walls and invade with fear and terror. If you try fighting your own battle, then God is not your defence. And so, the enemy can pull it down. **Psalm 94:22** tells us, 'But the Lord is my defence; and my God is the rock of my refuge'.

What do we do when we look around, and all we see is that we are surrounded by enemies? Take your eyes off the enemies! Yes, do take your eyes off the enemies and focus on the greatness of God. Focus on the Lord of Host.

Focus on His mighty power. Focus on the everlasting God and let Him reveal Himself to you. Let Him open your eyes to the mightiness of Him that surrounds you as His child. Let Him open your eyes to the mighty heavenly host surrounding your enemies.

STAY IN THE LIGHT

He did it before during the time of **Elisha in 2 Kings 6:13-18** where the king of Syria spied out Elisha and sent his great host after him. Elisha's servant became fearful at their sight, but Elisha assured him, *'Fear not, for they that be with us are more than they that be with them'*, and his eyes were opened to see the horses and chariots of fire that were for them.

Assuredly, we know that 'if God be for us, who can be against us?' (**Romans 8:31**); 'Nay, in all these things we are more than conquerors through Him that loved us' (**Romans 8:37**).

✚

PONDER ON THIS

Do you trust the Lord to direct your path?
Does your life reflect the faith you profess to have
in Him? Are you keeping your eyes on Jesus, the
author and perfecter of our faith (**Hebrews 12:2**)?

Personal Notes

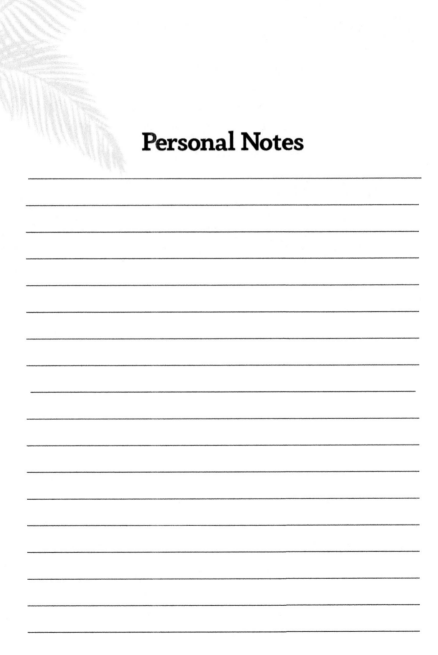

_____

_____

_____

_____

_____

_____

_____

_____

_____

_____

_____

_____

_____

_____

_____

_____

_____

_____

_____

_____

_____

Key Scriptures: *Exodus 14:10-12; Genesis 12;*
Psalm 44:6-7; Joshua 6: 20; Psalm 94:22; 2 Kings 6:13-18;
Romans 8:31; Romans 8:37; Hebrews 12:2

Week

2

Do You Love Me?

Jesus asked Simon Peter, 'Simon, son of Jonah, do you love me more than these?' Jesus asked him this question three times, and each time, He followed it by instructing Peter on what to do. The first time, He said, 'Feed my lambs'. the second time He said, 'Tend my sheep', and the third time, He said, 'Feed my sheep' (John 21:15-17 NKJV).

If you're expecting God to trust you with his work, then ask yourself, 'Do I love Jesus?' This is not a question to answer in a hurry because you may already have a default setting that gives an answer appropriated as being correct. You need to reflect on what it entails and, therefore, what it means to love Jesus.

How do you accurately follow and carry out the instructions of God if you do not love Him? **John 14:15** says, 'If you love me, keep my commandments'.

Therefore, we cannot effectively carry out the works of the Father without loving Him. Our love for God is a powerful force that spurs us on to do the will of the Father. God Himself demonstrated how the power of love moves us into action—the Bible says, *'For God so loved the world that He GAVE His only begotten son...'* (**John 3:16**). He was moved by love to sacrifice Himself for us.

That part of Himself is Jesus because **John 14:20** says, *'At that day you will know that I am in My Father, and you in Me, and I in you'.* God Himself demonstrated that to lay down one's self requires love. To give up everything and follow Jesus requires sacrificial love. To *'die'* to self and truly allow the Lordship of another over you requires love. To take up, believe, and follow His every command takes love.

John 14: 21 says *'He who has My commandments and keeps them, it is he who loves me. And he who loves Me will be loved by My Father, and I will love him and manifest Myself to him."* The joy derived from serving God stems from the love we have for Him and the desire to please Him.

That joy gives us strength when we would ordinarily have felt tired, weak, demotivated, disappointed, and wearied (**Nehemiah 8:10**).

I remember being a volunteer worker in a church I attended. The service I rendered was not in a department I would have chosen, but I decided to obey the request of the church leadership and became committed to the work.

Meetings would be held where conversations left me discouraged from continuing to serve; however, I always reminded myself of whom I was serving and why. I love Jesus and want to please God, so with the help of the Holy Spirit, I would be encouraged.

I wanted to render that service to God so much, so I kept my eyes on Him whom I love because He first loved me. I had to let my desire to please the Father overshadow all else. It was not always easy, but I have learnt, and continue to learn, that if I keep His commands, I can abide in His love (**John 15:10**). And it is this love that is the source of my love for Him (**1 John 4:19**).

Are you desiring for God to use you but unsure where to begin? Do you desire a closer walk with Him? Are you seeking how to reach and touch His heart?

Then you must answer the questions: Do you love Him? Are you continually loving Him? Are you passionate about Him?

You have to wholeheartedly accept His Lordship and totally submit to the supremacy of that Lordship. Start by confessing every displeasing way you have been living, then verbally confess your sins and every wrong doing.

Tell Him how truly sorry you are for those sins, and ask for his mercy. Ask Him to forgive you and help you not return to your displeasing ways. Ask Jesus to come into your life as your Lord and Saviour; tell Him that you accept and totally embrace His Lordship over your life. Ask God to please count you as one of His children and give you His Holy Spirit in Jesus' name.

If you have already accepted Jesus as your Lord and Saviour and desire a closer walk with Him, then you must begin to learn of Him and KNOW Him. We already have His word (the Bible), which tells us all about Him.

Spend time communing with Him through prayers and study His word to learn about Him. Meditate on His word so it becomes a part of you, and then do what it says.

Psalm 119:11 says, *'Your word I have hidden in my heart, That I might not sin against You.'* You need to wholeheartedly seek Him and study the Bible for you to be able to hide His word in your heart (**Psalm 119:9-10**).

Ask Him for understanding to learn His commandments (**Psalm 119:73**). **John 15:10-11** says, *'If you keep My commandments, you will abide in My love, just as I have kept My Father's commandments and abide in His love. These things I have spoken to you, that My joy may remain in you, and that your joy may be full'.*

Desiring a closer walk with God is akin to desiring a journey that takes you along the path to touch his heart. A journey where you learn of Him, get to know who He is, and discover the joy of reaching His heart.

To touch God's heart, it is not enough to accept His Lordship and stop there. It is not enough to study His word and stop there. You must exercise through faith what you have learnt of Him. You must DO as He commands.

You must be Christ-like and *'do'* as Jesus did. *'Most assuredly, I say to you, he who believes in Me, the works that I do he will do also; and greater works than these he will do, because I go to My Father'* (**John 14:12**). To do the will of the Father is to obey Him. And to obey, we need to trust Him to enable our faith because *'without faith, it is impossible to please God'* (**Hebrews 11:6**).

All our surrendering, seeking, obeying, trusting, and faith are built on our love for God.

To show His love for the Father, Jesus obeyed God's commandments: *'But that the world may know that I love the Father, and as the Father gave Me commandment, so I do. Arise, let us go from here'* (**John 14:31**).

To touch the heart of the Father, you must remain in love with Him, which transcends to doing his absolute will regardless of what it may cost.

❁

PONDER ON THIS

Now, pause and think about these questions:

Do you love Him? Are you continually loving Him? Are you passionate about Him?

Meditate on Revelation 2: 1-7 (CEV); verses 3 and 4 say, '*You have endured and gone through hard times because of me, yet you have not given up. But I have something against you! And it is this: You don't have as much love as you used to*'.

Do you love JESUS as you ought to? Ponder on this.

Personal Notes

_____

_____

_____

_____

_____

_____

_____

_____

_____

_____

_____

_____

_____

_____

_____

_____

_____

_____

_____

_____

Key Scriptures: *John 21:15-17 NKJV; John 14:15; John 3:16; John 14:20; John 14:21; Nehemiah 8:10; John 15:10; 1 John 4:19; Psalm 119:11; Psalm 119:9-10; Psalm 119:73; John 15:10-11; John 14:12; Hebrews 11:6; John 14:31; Revelation 2: 1-7*

Week

3

The Shackles That Bind

The shackles that bind the spirit, soul, and body. They wrap themselves around and engulf you till you're immersed in their totality. For example, the shackle of anger that bruises the heart and torments the mind until you can no longer function in positivity. It produces rage where control is lost; you just about contain it with human discipline.

However, with the help of the Holy Spirit, you stamp it underfoot until it is completely stumped out. *'It's not by power, nor by might but by the Spirit of the Lord'* (Zechariah 4:6).

When we are physically bruised or hurt, we feel pain and have different reactions. Some might wince or let out a cry, while others may weep from the pain and shout for help. The pain causes us to react. Anger stems from a 'bruise' on the inside.

It could be through something seen or heard or the outcome of an interaction or a situation. The *'pain'* from these stirs us up and we could respond by launching a direct attack on the source of pain. We may also seek relief by communicating with others who may have a soothing word for us, or we may be at the point where the fruit of the Spirit called self-control can manifest.

Whatever our reaction in those moments, we must know there will be some battles in the spirit. If anger is allowed to take hold, remain, and find a comfortable place in us, it invites its friends and family members—bitterness, unforgiveness and strife—which also bring with them all manner of evil (**James 3:16**).

Sometimes we may find it difficult to let go of the anger we feel. Like an accessory, we carry it around and even give it legitimacy by dwelling on how we have been deeply wronged, anchoring the blame on the perpetrator's neck.

We justify why it's okay to remain with that negativity when we are only allowing the festering of a wound. Our pride and ego have been inflicted with pain, and we need meekness, humility, patience, and long-suffering to manifest through the Holy Spirit's help.

The healing balm of Gilead may be required to soothe all hurt, and the blood of Jesus will cleanse all impurities that have accumulated from the anger.

As a very young Christian, I believed I could not be so offended as to hold a grudge for long. I unknowingly thought I had conquered anger until life's circumstances arose to thwart that thought.

Then, I realised I had ascribed my perceived ability to overcome anger to my doing and self-discipline—something achieved by myself. I had made it all about me. Afterwards, I began to rely on the Holy Spirit to help me, not only to overcome anger but also to overcome being easily offended and letting go of any grudges. The word of God that says it's not by might nor by power was revealed afresh, and I knew I needed the Spirit of God (**Zechariah 4:6**).

Anger makes the situation all about us. How I've been hurt. How I've been angered. How I've been bruised and betrayed.

We forget that there's a spirit behind the person. As children of God, committed to the Father's will and dedicated to serving Him, we have the Spirit of God living in us. However, are we allowing the Holy Spirit to constantly have His way? When we are not, what other spirit is having its way in us?

We must place upon ourselves a requirement to be crucified daily with Christ. We must allow 'I' to be nailed to the cross so that it is no longer 'I' that lives but Jesus living in me (**Galatians 2:20**).

Remember that there is a spirit behind the person so do not hate nor be malicious or unforgiving towards the person because it is the spirit in them stirring up and calling to wrestle with the spirit in you. '*For we wrestle not against flesh and blood, but against principalities, against powers, against the rulers of the darkness of this world, against spiritual wickedness in high places*' (**Ephesians 6:12**).

When we are aware of this, then we know that '*the weapons of our warfare are not carnal, but are mighty through God to the pulling down of strongholds*' (**2 Corinthians 10:3-6**).

We cannot combat or counteract the works of a spirit with the emotional response of the flesh—it will not work! Our Heavenly Father gave us an understanding that it is a spirit that can appeal to and penetrate another spirit.

The Bible says, *'For God is Spirit and they that must worship Him must do so in spirit and in truth'* (**John 4:24**). Only the deep calleth unto the deep (**Psalm 42:7**).

Call on your Heavenly Father to arise on your behalf and on behalf of the human vessel being used. Ask God to expel every spirit operating in darkness and churning out words and situations causing anger, strife, bitterness, malice, and all forms of evil.

The place of prayer is where we lovingly commune with our Heavenly Father. It is also a place of spiritual battles using the word of God and empowered by the Holy Spirit. When we pray using God's word, the Trinity is involved. We call on God the Father, through his word and son Jesus, empowered by the Holy Spirit.

So what do you do when you feel anger stirring or about to engulf you? PRAY! That may be the last thing you want to do, but pray. If you are struggling, get another child of God to pray for or with you.

Start by thanking God for all the wonderful things, people, and circumstances in your life. Thank Him for loving you in spite of your imperfections. Proceed to ask for mercy for all unconfessed sins, asking for grace to have total victory over them all. Tell your Heavenly Father how hurt you feel.

Choose to forgive and ask Him to help you soothe your hurt. Pray a blessing into the life of who caused the hurt. Ask for a deeper revelation of the love of God and a greater manifestation of the Holy Spirit in your life. Thank God for His patience towards you, and walk away in freedom. Be mindful that in many situations, you may have to live with reminders of that hurt, even confront it daily in some instances.

In the same vein, you must remember the requirement to be crucified with Christ daily. Crucifixion is not a short sharp death; it can be a long and painful experience before death occurs. We can see from the Holy Bible all that our Lord Jesus Christ went through before he got to the point where He said, *'It is finished'* (**John 19:30**). We are far from finished. To be truly Christ-like, we must be ready for all the trials that our Lord Jesus also went through.

We will be betrayed, bruised, wounded, and even feel forsaken, but we have been reassured that *'He will never leave nor forsake us'* (**Hebrews 13:5**). We may feel justified in our anger and want to hold on to it but we must remember not to sin while at it (**Ephesians 4:26-27**).

So the sooner we let it go the better for our all round health and wellbeing. Be justified by your faith in Christ Jesus (**Romans 5:1**).

Focus your mind and fix your eyes on the author and finisher of our faith. Jesus endured the cross for the joy that was before Him, so let us press on in our race towards the mark of eternal reward (**Hebrews 12:1-2; Philippians 3:13-15**).

Anger specialises in deprivation. It deprives us of total sanity, peace, rest, joy, the ability to overcome temptation, and, if you sin, access to the Father because if we regard iniquity in our hearts, the Lord will not hear us (**Psalm 66:18**).

Prayer releases the intense hold of anger, and the word of God sets us free from its power. Our daily surrender to the Lordship of Jesus gradually builds our immunity till we conquer anger: *'Nay in all these things we are more than conquerors through Christ who loves us'* (**Romans 8:37**).

✜

PONDER ON THIS

What shackles need shattering? Meditate on the word of God and pray through till you break through.

Personal Notes

_____

_____

_____

_____

_____

_____

_____

_____

_____

_____

_____

_____

_____

_____

_____

_____

_____

_____

_____

_____

_____

_____

Key Scriptures: *Zechariah 4:6; James 3:16; Galatians 2:20; Ephesians 6:12; 2 Corinthians 10:3-6; John 4:24; Psalm 42:7; John 19:30; Hebrews 13:5; Ephesians 4:26-27; Romans 5:1; Hebrews 12:1-2; Philippians 3:13-15; Psalm 66:18; Romans 8:37*

Week

4

Grace

The grace of God is just as it says, HIS grace. It belongs to Him; therefore, He can bestow it as and when He desires. The same goes for His mercy. The Bible says that He will have mercy on whom He will have mercy (**Exodus 33:19; Romans 9:15**). His grace contains the strength, ability, enablement, courage, and confidence to do what we ordinarily cannot do.

Paul said in **2 Corinthians 13:14**, '*May the grace of the Lord Jesus Christ, the love of God, and the fellowship of the Holy Spirit be with you all*'. The grace of God to us is a blessing for us, a blessing to be used for our good to His glory.

Therefore, we cannot choose to operate in our own strength and expect to use God's grace simultaneously, because the outcome of his grace is to give Him glory. *'I am the Lord; that is my name! I will not give my glory to anyone else, nor share my praise with carved idols'* (**Isaiah 42:8**).

It is either you choose to accept the strength that comes from God or from elsewhere; it is a choice! *'Choose you this day whom ye will serve'* (**Joshua 24:15**). To enjoy the grace of God, there is one major requirement—humility. **Proverbs 3:34** says, *'He has no use for conceited people, but shows favour to those who are humble.'* **James 4:6b** also says, *'God resists the proud, but gives grace to the humble'*, with a similar repetition in **1 Peter 5:5**.

Grace can be simplified as *'divine ability'*. This means it applies to every sphere of life where we need to *'do'*. Consequently, our very existence requires the grace of God— the grace to have the breath of God in us, to arise from our daily slumber, to mobilise ourselves and others and to do all that is needed from the rising of the sun to its going down.

The grace of God does not take away trials but enables us to overcome and supersede trials. The eagle and other birds of the sky encounter similar atmospheric conditions, but there is a grace given to the eagle to soar above storms.

Most birds find a place to hide or perch whilst waiting for the storm to pass. The eagle confidently flies into the fierce wind, using the current to gain speed and rise higher; its wings are made in a way that it locks so that its energy is conserved whilst using the pressure of the storm to glide.

Similarly, our daily experiences will bring along storms, but the grace of God ensures that we are not swallowed up, hiding, or so battered that we cannot continue. It encourages, refreshes, re-energises, and gives us the push in the way of confidence to go out and soar high.

Isaiah 40:31 says *'But those who trust in the Lord will find new strength. They will soar high on wings like eagles. They will run and not grow weary. They will walk and not faint.'*

It is by the grace of God that we receive forgiveness through Jesus Christ. That same grace is also made available so we do not abound in sin. *'Let us therefore come boldly to the throne of grace, that we may obtain mercy and find grace to help in time of need'* (**Hebrews 4:16**). *'Shall we continue in sin that grace may abound? God forbid!'* (**Romans 6:1-2**).

The grace that was made available to Jesus whilst he was on the earth which allowed Him to be without sin is also available to us (**Hebrews 4:15-16**). It is by grace that we are found, saved and reconciled to God.

By grace we *'grow in grace'* and in the knowledge of our Lord and Saviour Jesus Christ, as we have been instructed in **2 Peter 3:18**. His grace enables, and our gratitude for this enablement should be demonstrated by giving Him ALL the glory.

Are you able to fulfil your purpose, the essence of your calling, without the grace of God? Ponder on this.

'Then the Lord replied: Write down the revelation and make it plain on tablets so that a herald may run with it'. We have the grace to receive and run with God's vision for us (**Habakkuk 2:2**).

'...And let us run with perseverance the race marked out for us'. We have the grace to persevere (**Hebrews 12:1**).

'I have fought the good fight, I have finished the race, I have kept the faith'. We have the grace to finish well (**2 Timothy 4:7**).

Therefore, to successfully run our race and fulfil our purpose, we need the grace to receive the vision and run with it, to persevere through whatever may come, and to finish well to the glory of God.

The grace of God helps us to persevere, shapes our character, and gives us hope (**Romans 5:3-4**).

And so, the more of God's grace we have, the more we are shaped in the likeness of Christ and filled with Him—Christ in us, the hope of glory (**Colossians 1: 27**).

❖

PONDER ON THIS

As you ponder on these words, pray for more of God's grace in your life and always remember to give GLORY to God through your GRATITUDE for His GRACE.

Personal Notes

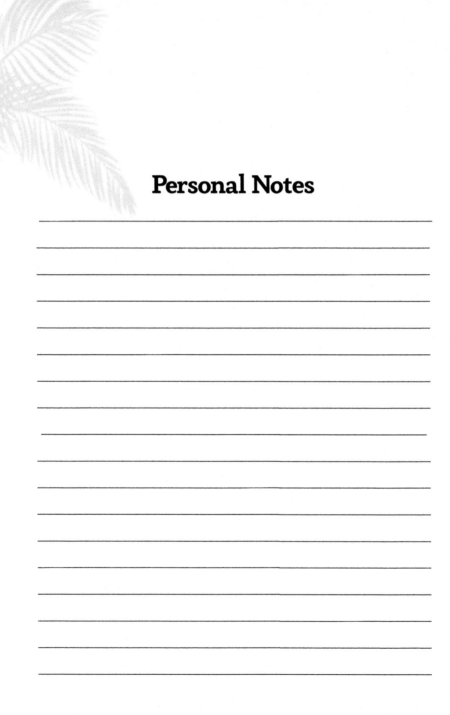

_____

_____

_____

_____

_____

_____

_____

_____

_____

_____

_____

_____

_____

_____

_____

_____

_____

_____

_____

_____

_____

Key Scriptures: *Zechariah 4:6; James 3:16; Galatians 2:20; Ephesians 6:12; 2 Corinthians 10:3-6; John 4:24; Psalm 42:7; John 19:30; Hebrews 13:5; Ephesians 4:26-27; Romans 5:1; Hebrews 12:1-2; Philippians 3:13-15; Psalm 66:18; Romans 8:37*

Waiting For Him

I was that Christian who prayed to God to reveal His purpose for my life. I was also that Christian who was quick to point out why I would be unable to achieve what the Lord was leading me to do. I would focus on my inability rather than His ability. By His mercy, God brought me to a place of realisation that it wasn't about me having everything figured out and planned with military precision.

It was about taking a step of faith to use whatever little I had been given for His glory whilst totally depending on Him. This required me not just to love God but also others with such compassion that I wanted to share 'my Jesus' with everyone.

I have not yet attained, so just like you, I am continually relying on the Spirit of God to teach and encourage me to step out and use my God-given gifts for His glory.

Let us briefly venture into Matthew chapter 25 together.

VERSES 1-13

What does the oil in the jar represent? This is our continuously renewed strength to remain in the Lord. This strength can be applied to our faith, love for Him, joy, and so on.

We only get this continuously renewed strength through His anointing upon our lives which we need in overflowing measure—an overflow of His goodness and mercy which allows us to forever dwell in His house and presence (Palm 23:5-6). How do we ensure we have oil in our jar, not just in our lamp?

VERSE 9

Go out and get wisdom! Out to where? Out to seek the Lord for wisdom because it is in wisdom that you find strength. A strong man is not necessarily wise, but a wise man is strong (Proverbs 24:3-5 NKJV).

You need the strength from God to keep watch. How do we keep watch? By staying alert, being on fire for Him, and acquiring wisdom to keep burning for God.

VERSES 14-30

Whilst waiting for the Lord to return, what are you doing with the thing or things He has deposited in you? Everyone has AT LEAST one talent. How are you occupying till He comes? How have you multiplied His gift(s) in your life? How have you brought about an increase to His kingdom?

Are you investing your gifts or sitting on them? It is not good enough to just be born again and then fall into a routine of church attendance, doing *'your bit'* as a worker, trying to be 'good' and staying 'good'. What profit are you bringing about to His kingdom? How are you being fruitful for Him?

How are you multiplying to the glory of His name (**Genesis 1:28**)? Will the Master have any account to settle with you when He returns? Have you been faithful with what you were given? Can you be entrusted with greater things? If you do not use what you have been given, then expect it to be taken away and given to the one that will put it to good use with results.

Verse 30 should encourage us not to become worthless servants. It is a position of no bearing, no direction, as there is no light to see where to go. There will be pain and regret when you're not living in purpose.

VERSES 31-46

If you are wondering, but I do not know my purpose. Start by praying for clarity of purpose, then begin to live a life that makes a difference.

Show the work in your faith **(James 2:14-17 NLT)**. How? Feed the hungry, give drinks to the thirsty, ask after the well-being of others, give to the poor, and encourage the sick and those who are lonely. Verse 40 helps us understand that when you start with at least one of these, you have begun doing something for the Lord. Some will say, but I'm surrounded by people who do not need these things.

Jesus said to Peter, *'Feed my sheep'* **(John 21:15-17)**. This means there are flocks in spiritual impoverishment as well. There is always someone whose need you can meet. You do not require a grand gesture; you only require a heart to do things for the Lord. As God sits in heaven, His desire for us is that our needs be met as we seek Him.

He wants us to replicate this desire towards one another. That way, His Kingdom can come and His will done on earth (**Matthew 6:10 NIV**).

God wants us to seek His kingdom, live righteously, and have our needs met (**Matthew 6:33 NLT**).

❖

PONDER ON THIS

Have you surrendered your talents and gifts to God? If so, how are you using them for Him? Do you seek for Him to renew your strength? Are you staying alert to the opportunities He brings, enabling you to use your talent for His glory? Do not let life pass you by. Seek and hold on to the purposes of God for you.

Personal Notes

_____

_____

_____

_____

_____

_____

_____

_____

_____

_____

_____

_____

_____

_____

_____

_____

_____

_____

_____

_____

_____

_____

Key Scriptures: Matthew 25:1-46; Psalm 23:5-6; Proverbs 24:3-5; Genesis 1:28; James 2:14-17; John 21:15-17; Matthew 6:10; Matthew 6:33

Week

6

Heritage

There are occasions that have caused me to reflect on certain thoughts or actions. In doing this, I asked myself these questions: Do these thoughts and actions showcase the nature of Christ in me? Have I allowed myself conform to this world through my conversations and actions? Does my countenance denote my spiritual heritage?

Do you ever ask yourself similar questions? Let us briefly delve into **Psalm 78.** The children of Israel did not understand their heritage. They took for granted all God had done for their ancestors and themselves.

They did not realise how precious they were to the Holy One of Israel, and as a result, they suffered numerous losses.

God, in His mercy, always drew them back to Himself. By not understanding the importance of their heritage, there was a *'reshuffling'*, and Judah was chosen over Ephraim. This was after Israel lost the battle to the Philistines, and the Ark of God was captured in **1 Samuel 4.**

This loss was a result of Israel building shrines to other gods. They forgot that God was their rock, that the Most High was their redeemer. They rejected God and did not allow His nature to dwell in them.

Our Spiritual heritage is what we inherit as children of God. This is passed down to us as joint heirs with Christ. It constitutes our identity and imprints heavily on our sense of self. So, what is my spiritual heritage? Find these out by asking, 'What is the nature of God?' Who God is. Once you do, you will know what heritage is yours as a spirit being, because remember that God is Spirit and all those who worship Him must do so in spirit and truth.

In spirit, to be able to connect. In truth, because there's no imperfection (no lie) in His nature, and we must approach Him with such reverence. God is not a man, that He should lie... (**Numbers 23:19**).

Your heritage comes with birth; therefore, have you been birthed in God by confessing and repenting from your sins, accepting Jesus as your Lord and Saviour; and living life to the evidence that you're indeed a child of God? When you live a Christ-like life with the understanding that you're joint heirs with Christ Jesus, you are assured to also have access to what Jesus can access.

Study the life of Jesus whilst on earth and know the way you're expected to live, the nature you're to take on, not in pretence but through a deep connection with the Heavenly Father. Do this by studying the word of God, meditating on it, praying it, and professing the heart of the Father by the help of the Holy Spirit.

The more time we spend in His presence, the better we understand His nature and, therefore, know what is expected of us. We begin to reflect His character and consciously put it on so that all we do daily is encapsulated in Him. After all, *'in Him we live, move and have our being'* (**Acts 17:28**).

This was how we were originally designed to live so that the daily chronicles of our lives as God's children reflect His very nature. This way, we are identifiable by what our spirit man represents—the family of God. We, therefore, display the uniqueness, values, traditions, culture, etcetera of this family that has been passed down through our 'God family' which we read about in the Bible.

When we follow the *'ethos'*, commands, and expectations of our *'God family'*, all men shall know to whom we belong by the heritage we portray. 'A new commandment I give to you, that you love one another; as I have loved you, that you also love one another.

By this all will know that you are My disciples, if you have love for one another' (**John 13:34-35 NKJV**).

Which spiritual lineage are you identifiable with? What characteristic displays qualify you for this line of heritage? What characteristic displays disqualifies you from this line of heritage? *'Displays'* are not just your physical acts but also the 'acts of your mind'.

What do your imaginations and thoughts display? *'Finally, brethren, whatever things are true, whatever things are noble, whatever things are just, whatever things are pure, whatever things are lovely, whatever things are of good report, if there is any virtue and if there is anything praiseworthy—meditate on these things'* (**Philippians 4:8 NKJV**).

❖

PONDER ON THIS

How do you plan to ensure that the very nature of God dwells in you? Prayerfully meditate on these Bible verses:

• *'But his delight is in the law of the LORD, And in His law he meditates day and night'* **(Psalms 1:2 NKJV)**.

• *'This Book of the Law shall not depart from your mouth, but you shall meditate in it day and night, that you may observe to do according to all that is written in it. For then you will make your way prosperous, and then you will have good success'* **(Joshua 1:8 NKJV)**.

Personal Notes

_____

_____

_____

_____

_____

_____

_____

_____

_____

_____

_____

_____

_____

_____

_____

_____

_____

_____

_____

_____

_____

_____

_____

_____

_____

_____

_____

_____

_____

_____

_____

_____

_____

_____

_____

_____

_____

_____

_____

Key Scriptures: *Psalm 78; 1 Samuel 4; Numbers 23:19; Acts 17:28; John 13:34-35; Philippians 4:8; Psalm 1:2; Joshua 1:8*

Week

7

Great God

'Greater is He that is in me than he that is in the world'. This is one of my fast-acting spiritual capsules. It relieves hurtful situations, encourages me at the brink of giving up, and reminds me of my spiritual heritage. The whole verse says:

'Ye are of God, little children, and have overcome them: because greater is he that is in you, than he that is in the world' (**1 John 4:4 KJV**).

This verse is the *'Vitamin D'* that allows the *'Calcium'* of **Ephesians 3:14-21** to further take effect in my inner man. Let's take a quick look at its effectiveness.

Read Ephesians 3:14-21.

Who is in you? God.

Why is He great? He is the Father of our Lord Jesus Christ and the creator of everything in heaven and on earth. Therefore, He is greater than everything He has created.

How do we ensure we indeed have His greatness in us? We know that God is able to grant us the riches of His glory according to verse 16. This allows us to be strengthened, empowered with might, and inner strength through His Spirit.

To be strengthened in the inner man, it is not enough to say the prayer of repentance, give our lives to Christ, and attend church services.

Even though these are of utmost importance and the beginning of a new life with Christ living in us. The Bible says *'Whosoever shall confess that Jesus is the Son of God, God dwelleth in him, and he in God'* (1 John 4:15 KJV).

We must have faith—we must trust Him—not just by word of mouth but by our daily interaction with Him and our daily actions that show our constant transformation through His word.

We must take root in Him by spending quality time in His presence, in His word, and in the worship of Him. This helps our spirit to connect with God's Spirit, be deeply connected to His love, and stay strong in Him.

To be strengthened in the inner man, we need to spend time in the place of prayer. We need to pray for understanding, to know how wide, long, high and deep God's love is towards us. And although verse 18 says Christ's love is too great to fully understand, we should also pray to continually experience it. **Verse 19** goes on to say, *'Then you will be made complete with all the fullness of life and power that comes from God'*.

When we totally surrender ourselves, become yielded to the Holy Spirit, and allow God to fill us with His power, we will begin to see the great move of God in our lives. We will begin to see His power manifesting in all that concerns us. **Verse 20** assures us that *'God is able, through His mighty power at work within us to accomplish infinitely more than we might ask or think'*.

The **New King James Version** says He *'is able to do exceedingly abundantly above all that we ask or think, according to the power that works in us'*. God can exceed all our imaginations and expectations, and he can do so in overflowing measure (**Ephesians 3:20**), which means He won't just exceed your expectations and imagination once or twice; He can do it continuously... over and over again. When the power of God is within us, when we are filled with God's greatness, things beyond our imaginations begin to happen.

When we give all glory to God, ascribing greatness to Him; He shows us that He is indeed the all powerful God.

✦

PONDER ON THIS

With the above, we go beyond confessing and encouraging ourselves with the Bible verse *'greater is He that is in me than he that is in the world'* to living as the images of God, filled with His power, knowing that most assuredly, with every certainty, *'greater is He that is in us than he that is in the world'* (**1 John 4:4 KJV**).

Do you truly believe this? Meditate on 1 John 4:4.

Personal Notes

_____

_____

_____

_____

_____

_____

_____

_____

_____

_____

_____

_____

_____

_____

_____

_____

_____

_____

_____

_____

_____

_____

Key Scriptures: *1 John 4:4; Ephesians 3:14-21;
1 John 4:15*

Testimonies

Write down the impact of this devotional guide on your daily walk with God. Think of one or more testimonies for each week of reading this guide.

WEEK 1

WEEK 2

_____

_____

_____

_____

_____

_____

_____

_____

_____

_____

_____

_____

_____

_____

_____

_____

_____

_____

_____

_____

WEEK 3

WEEK 4

WEEK 5

_____

_____

_____

_____

_____

_____

_____

_____

_____

_____

_____

_____

_____

_____

_____

_____

_____

_____

_____

WEEK 6

WEEK 7

_____

_____

_____

_____

_____

_____

_____

_____

_____

_____

_____

_____

_____

_____

_____

_____

_____

_____

_____

_____

_____

Printed in Great Britain
by Amazon

29139458R00051